# Companion Journal

by Constance Messmer

© 2026 Constance Messmer

Also by CONSTANCE MESSMER

Soul Yoga

Soul Yoga: Inspiration Cards

Your 11 Soul Senses: A Journal for Self-Discovery

Some Dogs Talk

Blocks


For detailed lectures on each of Your 12 Chakras,
join me on The Constance Messmer Podcast.

<u>Disclaimer</u>

The material in this book is intended for educational purposes only. Neither this material nor the techniques should be viewed as medical advice. It is not meant for diagnosing or treating health conditions. If you or your pet has a health concern, consult a licensed healthcare provider or veterinarian. No guarantees or liabilities are accepted regarding the effects of following the recommendations provided.

Copyright © 2026 by Constance Messmer

All rights reserved. No part of this work may be reproduced in whole or in part, stored in a retrieval system, or transmitted in any form by any means – electronic, mechanical, or other – without written permission from the author, except by a reviewer, who may quote brief passages in a review.

Dedication & Acknowledgements

This soul spelunking journal comes from my path to yours. I dedicate it to the beautiful exploration of your chakras. May you come to understand yourself in profound and new ways.

It is with deep gratitude that I wish to thank and acknowledge the help of two lovely pals, journeying alongside me:

*Abby Remer*
Thanks for exploring the deeper meaning of my words and instructions, pulling the best parts together for traveling ease.
I appreciate our pace and your company on this voyage together.

*Tarra Corcoran*
For your gifts of detail and countless hours of brainstorming reworks before my concepts could even land on the printed page.
I adore you more than words can reveal.

LOVE,

*Constance* ♥

Your chakras are repositories of soul information.
For a map of your life, look to your chakras.

Constance Messmer

Dear One,

I'm so glad we found each other!

This journal was created with you in mind. My work is to empower you to a deeper understanding of yourself and choices on a profound and personal level.

Working through your 12 chakras are pathways to that greater encounter.

Life experiences are stored in the energy fields of your chakras. Once you recognize these centers are there to explore, your world opens to the benefits of both struggle and strengths. Information gives way to options for what you can do to change anything to your advantage.

I've been at this study for decades. (And more than likely, a multitude of lifetimes.) So, what you have in your hands is a map of potential sites where you might want to pause and ponder.

This 12-chakra Journal is designed to document your journey of self-discovery. Use it at your own pace and refer to it annually or before embarking on something new. I invite you to use the journaling prompts I've provided, as well as explore what comes up with your own deliberations. Putting findings down on paper helps to remember where you've been and where you'd like to be headed.

The moments on the journey do not define you. They are meant to inspire you.

You can use this book as a standalone journal or alongside my book, *Soul Yoga*. In that book, you'll find a deeper understanding of your chakra system, using your 12 chakras as a map to reaching your highest potential.

I also have *Soul Yoga: Inspiration Cards* based on my work with your 12 chakras. They offer soul whisperings from the cosmos to remind you of who you are and what you are capable of.

The journey of life is yours. How you choose to live it is up to you. For your benefit and that of the world we all live in, I hope to offer you insight, because as you grow and expand, that radiance will shine outward and touch us all.

Make your lifetime a conscious journey.

I'm grateful for you!
Big LOVE!

This book covers the following twelve major chakras: Earth, Root, Sacral, Solar Plexus, Heart, Throat, Brow, Crown, Higher Self, Karmic, Cosmic, and Divine.

Each section provides a brief overview of the chakra, its location, and journaling prompts to help guide your exploration. Blank pages are included for your journaling experience.

## Let us begin...

# Your 12 Chakras

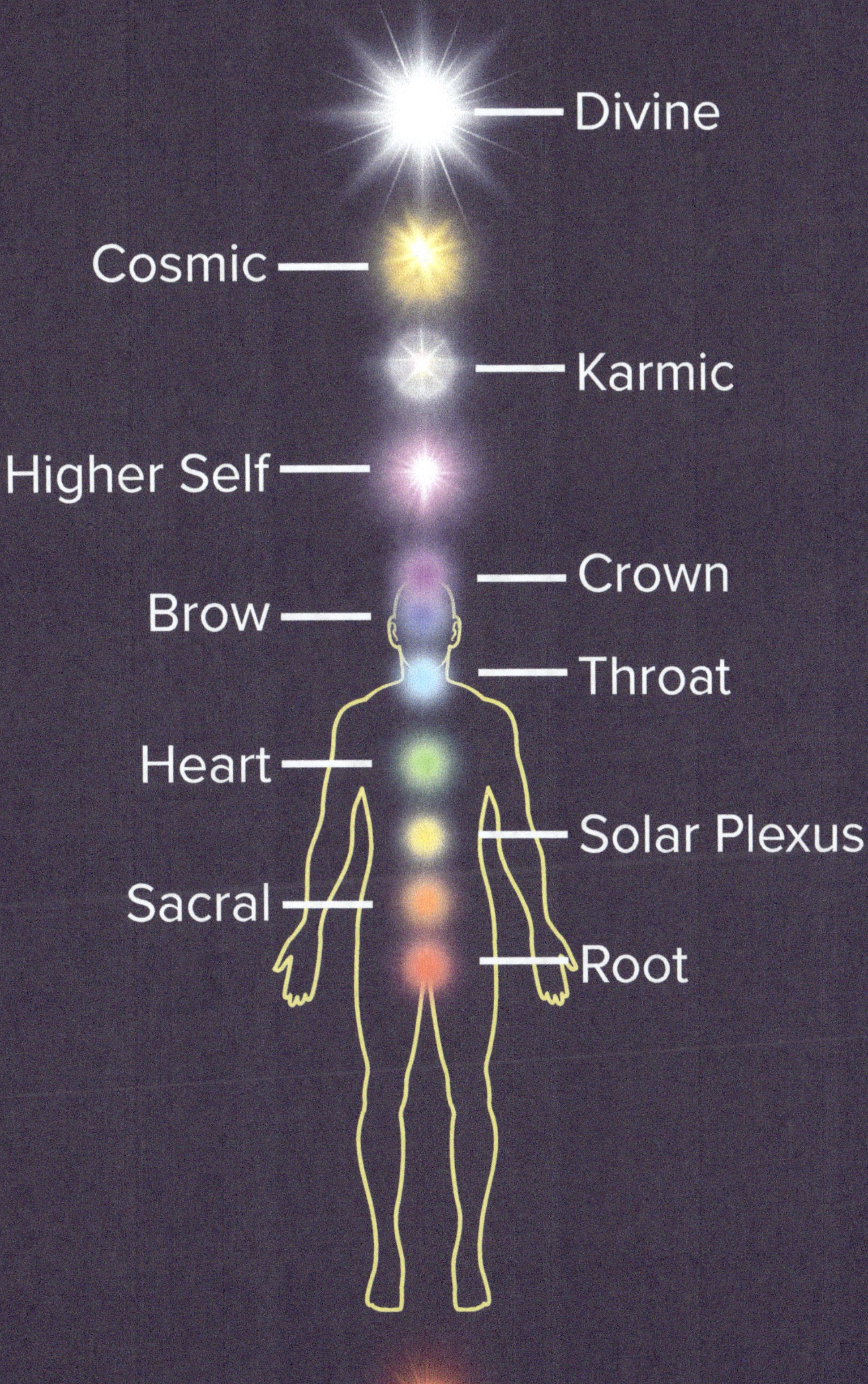

# Earth Chakra

*Survival*

Your connection to your life and to all life on the earth. Ability to ground your energy. Ability to be physically present.

Location: A foot or so beneath the soles of the feet.

Journal Prompts:

- As you contemplate your connection to your life and to all life on Earth, what comes up for you?

- What do you notice about feeling grounded compared to feeling lightheaded or out of your body, especially when pondering your connection to the earth and the energy flowing down and through the soles of your feet?

- How are you showing up in your life right now?

- To what degree do you stand your own ground?

- What practice, outlook, or approach might help you stay connected to your life and all life on Earth?

*You are an integral part of this world.*

# Root Chakra

*Foundation*

Safety issues. Basic survival needs being met: food, shelter, clothing.

Location: At the very base of the spine, the coccyx.

Journal Prompts:

- When you bring awareness to the base of your spine and breathe, do you feel supported in your life?

- When you bring awareness to the base of your spine and breathe, do you feel safe in your life?

- Which basic needs—food, shelter, clothing, daily safety—are asking for attention right now, and what small, practical step would help you feel more secure?

- As you mentally scan down each leg, what arises around mother issues on the left and father issues on the right, and how might these patterns be influencing your Root Chakra today?

- What would empower you to successfully "stand on your own two feet"?

*Feed your body & soul with complete goodness.*

# $S$acral Chakra

*Sexuality, Relationships, Creativity, New Beginnings*
Represents your connection to relationships,
sexual issues, creativity, and new beginnings.

Location: About two inches below the navel.

Journal Prompts:

- What are you noticing about how sexuality, relationships, creativity, or new beginnings are showing up in your life right now?

- How do you want to befriend your sexuality or creativity?

- When you place one hand on the front of your lower belly and one on your lower back, what sensations, feelings, or gut instincts do you notice about a current relationship or commitment?

- As you consider money, work, or a new venture, what do you notice in your lower back or belly, and what does that indicate about the next right step in your interactions and ethics?

- What relationships have you outgrown, and what new ones would you like to form?

*Every day choose to do something you love.*

# Solar Plexus Chakra

*Personal Power*

Self-esteem. Who you are. What you came to do.

Location: Between the navel and the heart.

Journal Prompts:

- When an interaction or thought "hits you in your gut," what feelings do you notice first, and what do they reveal about your truth and the step you need to take to honor it right now?

- As you consider your mental chatter and how you meet your needs, where do you observe shifts in self-esteem and personal power? What would living, embodying, and speaking your truth look like today in terms of connecting with your authentic self?

- With one or both hands on your solar plexus, what are you meant to hold on to and what are you meant to let go of?

- When you tune into this power center, what guidance do you receive about being in charge of your life and following your dreams?

- What have you come to do in this lifetime?

*Honor your soul senses.*

# Heart Chakra

*Center of Love*

Ability to give and receive love.

Location: Center of the chest, in line with the heart.

Journal Prompts:

- Placing your hands and attention on your heart center, do you notice any grief, resentment, or loneliness clouding your heart? What shifts occur when you ask your soul for a deeper understanding about what's coming up for you and what you might do to bring awareness, acceptance, balance, or change?

- Reflect on feelings of being loved/unloved or wanted/unwanted and any family patterns you're aware of that may be causing or impacting these feelings. What do you observe in your upper back, shoulders, arms, or hands, and what small action would help you course-correct back to love today?

- Do you love what you do for work, service, or volunteer efforts? These, too, influence the energy of your Heart Chakra. What needs to change, if anything?

- When you place your hands on your chest, note your initial emotional responses. What do they reveal about your current ability to give and receive love?

- Now, in the center of this knowing, become aware of the inner wisdom of your heart's truth. What are your next steps toward personal understanding, self-compassion, self-love, and joy?

*Acknowledge your emotions.*

# Throat Chakra

*Communication and Trust*

Speaking your truth. Listening. Trust issues. Speaking and Hearing experiences.

Location: Throat and mouth area. Ears.

Journal Prompts:

- Where in your life are you being asked to speak your truth?

- As you place your hands on your throat and ask what's in here and what it needs, what emotions or memories surface about communication?

- When you contemplate your truth—how you want to speak it, what you want to do, who you want to do it with—what commitments, mental chatter, or relationships are ready for clearer, cleaner, more honest communication?

- Do you listen for the sake of understanding, or do you listen to respond? And what shifts within you when you slow down to listen for comprehension before you respond?

- In what areas of your life do you wish you were a better communicator and what would be your first steps in doing so?

*Honor your authentic truth.*

# Brow Chakra

*Knowledge and Wisdom*
Center of consciously processing intellectual and psychic awareness and impressions.

Location: An inch above the point between the eyebrows.

Journal Prompts:

- What do you observe about how your mind interprets your psychic impressions—and how does that inform your next right step?

- Where are you being asked to know and honor yourself in planning, decision-making, or learning from experience?

- What shifts when you listen to your psychic nudges without letting mental chatter talk you out of it?

- What must you do to honor your psychic strengths?

- What can you do to increase your peace of mind today?

*Don't let your mind talk you out of your greatness.*

# $C$rown Chakra

*Inspiration and Mysticism*
Center of claircognizance (knowing) and opening to the upper chakras beyond the physical body.

Location: Top of the head. If you were to place your thumbs in your ears and bring your middle fingers to the top of your head, the meeting point of your fingertips is the Crown Chakra point.

Journal Prompts:

- As you bring awareness to the very top of your head, what do you notice about inspiration, clear knowing, or a sense of connection that might be flowing to you right now?

- Where are you tempted to shut the door on a spiritual experience?

- What changes when you hold spiritual encounters as sacred—perhaps by journaling—rather than negating them?

- When it comes to your values, decisions, or ability to trust life, what updates are asking for your attention and reconsideration?

- What larger pattern of life and your part in it is being revealed to you lately?

*Don't let your mind talk you out of your greatness.*

# **H**igher Self Chakra

*Higher Consciousness*
Connection to Spirit, Interconnectedness

Location: Within your auric field, just above your Crown Chakra. Each of the four Upper Chakras is stacked above the crown of your head at evenly spaced distances from one another. (On me, they are four inches apart.) To help you locate yours, reach your hands up above you. Your fingertips will reach your Divine Chakra. The rest align below, evenly spaced apart.

Journal Prompts:

- As you bring awareness to the space just above the top of your head, what do you notice about messages, insights, or shifts in perception that feel like they're coming through your higher self-connection?

- Where are you beginning to differentiate between your ego self and higher self in your choices and words?

- When living from your higher consciousness, what do you observe about the ripple effects in your life and relationships?

- What limiting belief patterns might be holding you back from your path of higher conscious living?

- What truth or clarity is your higher self asking you to honor?

*Your soul senses awaken
you to the wisdom of your higher self.*

# Karmic Chakra

*Soul Path and Karmic Journey*
Akashic Records

Location: Above the top of the head, beyond the Higher Self Chakra. Remember, each of the four Upper Chakras is stacked above the crown of your head at evenly spaced distances from one another. (On me, they are four inches apart from each other.) To help you source your location, reach your hands up above you, your fingertips will reach your Divine Chakra. The rest align below, evenly spaced apart. Beneath your Divine Chakra is your Cosmic Chakra, beneath that is your Karmic Chakra.

## Journal Prompts:

- As you look back on pivotal moments and the relationships or connections you couldn't shake, what patterns do you notice that might reflect soul promises, vows, or karmic ties in your life path today?

- What obligations or goals that you set for this life are asking you for your attention now?

- Do you sense unhappiness reverberating when you don't pursue what you know you came to do? What is your first step toward your true path?

- When you consider wounds and strengths that feel older than your lifetime, what do you observe about how they permeate your life and energy?

- What support would help you trust life and see the larger pattern at play to support your every step?

*Purify your karma with conscious connections to choices.*

# Cosmic Chakra

*Cosmic Consciousness*
You begin to see that you are an integral part of the universe

Location: Each of the four Upper Chakras is stacked above the crown of your head at evenly spaced distances from one another. (On me, they are four inches apart from each other.) To source your location, reach your hands up above you, your fingertips will reach your Divine Chakra. The rest align below, evenly spaced apart. There, beneath the Divine Chakra and above your Karmic Chakra, you will find your Cosmic Chakra.

Journal Prompts:

- When you notice that you are glimpsing or living from cosmic consciousness, what do you observe about feeling like an integral part of the universe?

- Where are values, ethics, and unity with all things inviting you to see the larger pattern and to trust life today?

- If the confines of ego consciousness are present, what supportive space or simple offering—such as prayer for others—would help you validate your higher awareness and make a difference?

- How can you hold space for others with whom you don't align?

- Where in your life are you being called to a greater sense of community?

*You matter.*

# Divine Chakra

*Divine Consciousness*
Realm of true spiritual essence, your core consciousness

Location: Reach your hands up above you, your fingertips will reach your Divine Chakra; it extends upwards from there.

Journal Prompts:

- As you bring awareness to the space above the top of your head, what do you notice about entering that blissful, illuminating state of being one with Source energy?

- How does being one with Source move you to live your life today?

- Which spiritual practice is calling you: sacred dance, yoga, art, song or music, prayer, meditation, or sitting in spirit?

- What shifts as you give your spiritual practice your undivided attention to recognize the frequency that is pure Source and Divine Consciousness?

- When the resonance becomes overwhelming or brings tears, what helps you maintain the vibration and master your focus so you can walk and permeate Divine Consciousness?

*You are divine!*

# So, there you have it
# –your wonderful self!

I applaud you for working your way through
your 12 chakras.
This practice is like yoga for your soul, inspiring union.
This is always here for you to return. Home. To you.

# Thanks for Tuning In!

Constance Messmer is a Transformational Speaker and leader in human potential. With decades of experience in practice and teaching, she has become a trusted guide for those seeking to unlock their innate potential.

Her journey began early in life, as she discovered and honed her abilities to connect with the spirit world. Through dedicated work with both spirit and clients, Messmer has cultivated a profound understanding of human interaction and potential.

Guided by the highest source energy and a commitment to what is best for all, Messmer's mission is clear: to spread her message far and wide, connecting individuals with their innate abilities and fostering a journey in higher conscious living and human evolution.

Newsletter Sign Up:  ConstanceMessmer.com

The Constance Messmer Podcast: Wherever you listen to podcasts or on **youtube.com/constancemessmer**

Social: Instagram, Facebook, LinkedIn @constancemessmer